KILLER NATURE!

Beastly Bugs

Lynn Huggins-Cooper

W

FRANKLIN WATTS
LONDON • SYDNEY

First published in 2005 by Franklin Watts
96 Leonard Street, London EC2A 4XD

Franklin Watts Australia
Hachette Children's Books
Level 17/207 Kent Street, Sydney NSW 2000

Editor: Jennifer Schofield
Art Director and Jacket Designer: Peter Scoulding
Designer: Jay Young
Picture researcher: Diana Morris

Acknowledgements:
Ingo Arndt/FLPA: front cover cl. Ingo Arndt/Nature PL: 6. Stephen
Ausmus/ARS/USDA: 14. Barb Backes: 29. Anthony Bannister/NHPA:
front cover bl, 10. Scott Bauer/ARS/USDA: 5, 13. Scott Bauer/USDA/
ARS/insectimages.org: 12. Mark Edwards/Still Pictures: 22b.
FogdenPhotos.com: 1, 25.Gautier/Still Pictures: 18. Wernher Krutein/
Photovault: 15. Dennis Kunkel/OSF: 21. E.K.Lorenz/SPL: 28. Ken Preston-
Mafham/Premaphotos:11,16. Rod Preston-Mafham/Premaphotos: 24.
Jack Milchanowski/Ecoscene: front cover r, 26, 27. OSF: 4, 17, 19.
Peter Oxford/Nature PL: 7. Hans Pfletschinger/Still Pictures: 20.
Kjell Sandved/Ecoscene: 9. Jane Shemilt/SPL: 22cl. Sinclair Stammers/SPL: 23.

Every attempt has been made to clear copyright.
Should there be any inadvertent omission please
apply to the publisher for rectification.

A CIP catalogue record for this book
is available from the British Library.

ISBN: 0 7496 6099 6
Dewey Classification: 595.7

Printed in China

Contents

Beastly bugs

Insects and other creepy crawlies are all around us. Scientists believe that there are nearly 8.5 million species of bug in the world, including insects and arachnids. In this book, we look at some of the more beastly bugs around.

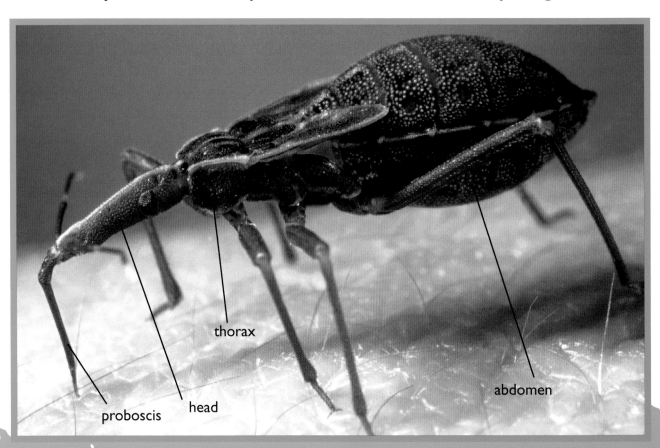

proboscis   head   thorax   abdomen

Bug facts

All insects have six legs. Their bodies are made up of three parts – the head, thorax and abdomen. Most insects start life as an egg. Once they hatch, they go through a few changes before they become adults.

Arachnids have eight legs and two parts to their bodies. Arachnids do not go through the same changes as insects do before they become adults. Instead, arachnids – such as the scorpions in this book – moult, or shed their skin.

Friend or foe?

There are many harmless bugs in the world, such as fireflies and ladybirds. But not all bugs are this friendly.

Dangerous killer bugs such as Africanised bees (left), bark scorpions and mosquitoes can sting, bite, and cause deadly diseases such as malaria.

Can you tell the difference between a harmless bug and a killer creepy crawly? Read on to find out more about these minibeasts – it just might save your life one day!

Spiky puss caterpillars

The puss caterpillar is the larva of the flannel moth. These fluffy-looking creepy crawlies are found in the southern states of the USA – Texas, Maryland, Florida and Missouri – and in Mexico. They are herbivores and they feed on the leaves of elm, oak, plum, rose, wild cherry, holly and sycamore trees.

Fact!

In Mexico, these furry bugs are called *el perrito* which means 'little dog'.

Vital statistics

Puss caterpillars are quite small. They grow up to only 3.6 centimetres long. They are covered in long, silky hairs.

Under the hairs are short, hollow spikes. If you touch the hairs, the spikes break off into your skin, injecting venom.

When caterpillars sting

Out of 50 types of stinging caterpillar found in the USA, puss caterpillars are the most poisonous. However, they use their poisonous spikes to protect themselves rather than to attack other animals. Puss caterpillars can sting even when they are dead, so that other animals avoid them.

More about puss caterpillars

Encounters with people

People who touch puss caterpillars are in for a painful surprise. Once the spikes have injected their poison, there is a burning feeling and the sting starts to swell. The victim may also have cramps, a headache, fever and feel like vomiting. If you are stung by one of these nasty bugs, you should wash the irritated area as soon as possible. This will take away any spikes and poison that are left in the skin. Holding ice on the area will help with the pain and swelling.

Fact!

The painfulness of a sting depends on the caterpillar's size – bigger caterpillars have more painful stings.

Survival

Puss caterpillars are not endangered. In Texas, USA, in 1923 and 1954, there were very large numbers of caterpillars and many people were stung. There may have been so many caterpillars because there were low numbers of predators, such as birds, during those years.

Life cycle of a caterpillar

In the late spring or early summer, flannel moths lay eggs on leaves. After a few days, larvae hatch from the eggs. Within weeks, the larvae grow into hairy puss caterpillars. The caterpillars do not build cocoons (silky coverings). Instead, they change into moths inside their own skin. When this happens, the caterpillars look dead – but they are in fact pupating (changing from a caterpillar pupa to a moth). The caterpillars stay like this through the winter. In spring, they break out of their old skin as adult moths.

Stinging Africanised bees

In 1956, fierce African bees were taken to Brazil to breed with European honey bees. Beekeepers hoped the new Africanised bees would make more honey than European bees in Brazil's hot weather.

The Africanised bees were accidentally released into the wild. They have spread quickly. In 1990, they were found in the USA in Texas, and by 1999, they had spread as far as California.

Vital statistics

Africanised honey bees look similar to European bees, but they are a little smaller. They are about 2 centimetres long. Only the female worker bees have a poisonous stinger on their abdomen. These bees live together in groups called colonies. They also swarm out together to find pollen and nectar.

Encounters with people

Africanised honey bees are not more poisonous than European bees, they are just more likely to attack. The bees are also easily disturbed – the sound of a lawn mower nearby is enough to make them attack.

Fact!
Africanised bees are fast fliers. They can reach amazing speeds of up to 24 kph.

More about killer bees

When bees attack

Africanised honey bees are known for attacking people. They are also called killer bees. Often, hundreds of killer bees can swarm out to sting at the same time. Beekeepers wear gloves and masks because the bees sting several times once they have a victim.

Killer bees can chase their victims for up to 800 metres before stinging them. The stings are quite painful and they can be fatal for people who are allergic to bee stings. They can also be deadly for young or elderly people who cannot always escape fast enough.

Real-life stories

In 1991, Jesus Diaz from Texas, USA was attacked while mowing his lawn. He escaped with eighteen stings. Another victim was not so lucky. In 1993, 82-year-old Lino Lopez died on his ranch. He was stung 40 times as he removed a colony of bees from a wall.

Survival

Africanised bees are not endangered – in fact they are spreading fast. Each year, they spread another 320 kilometres. Africanised bees can travel up to 80 kilometres to form new colonies and to find food. The European bees usually move only a couple of kilometres.

Life cycle of a bee

Africanised honey bees grow from egg to adult quicker than European honey bees. Each colony has one queen bee. It is her job to lay eggs in cells made of beeswax. She can lay an amazing 1,500 eggs each day. About three days after being laid, the eggs develop into larvae. The larvae look like rice. They have no legs, wings, antennae or eyes. They feed for a few days before becoming pupae. It takes just three weeks for the pupae to become adult bees.

Ferocious fire ants

Fire ants were originally from South America. Now, they are found across the world in warm and tropical places, such as parts of the USA, Africa and Asia. There are several different species of fire ant and it is hard to tell the difference between them and house or garden ants.

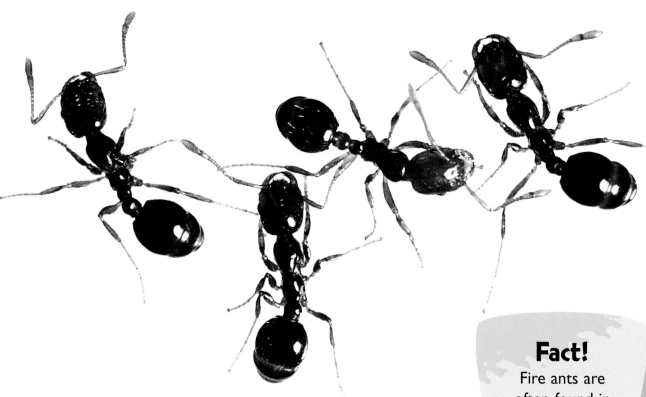

Vital statistics

Fire ants are a red-brown colour. They are small creatures, about 2–6 millimetres long. The worker ants in each colony build tall, dome-shaped mounds along roadsides and on farmland. There can be an amazing 500,000 worker ants in each colony.

Fact!

Fire ants are often found in air conditioners. They can eat through the wires and cause fires.

Survival

Fire ants are very common – often they can infest an area. They are hard to get rid of because the pesticides used to kill them do not always work.

Life cycle of a fire ant

The queen ant lays eggs. She can lay up to 800 eggs a day. The eggs hatch in six to ten days. After this, the larvae pupate. Adult fire ants emerge up to 15 days later.

How they kill

Fire ants eat carrion. They will also kill insects and small animals. These nasty bugs have even been known to attack foals and calves that are too young to run away. The ants kill by hanging on with their sharp jaws as they use their stingers to inject venom into their prey.

When fire ants sting

Fire ants get their name because their stings burn. The sting causes an itchy blister that can easily become infected. Many fire ants can attack at the same time. Since the 1930s, these vicious minibeasts have killed about 60 people in the USA.

Deadly assassin bugs

There are many different species of assassin bug. They are found from South America to North America, Africa and Australia. They are also known as kissing bugs because they pierce the lips, eyelids and ears of their prey.

Vital statistics

Assassin bugs have flat bodies and small, cone-shaped heads. Average adults are about 2 centimetres long but they may grow up to 5 centimetres. These stinging insects have a long, sharp proboscis which they use to stab their victims' skin.

Life cycle of an assassin bug

Female assassin bugs lay their eggs usually near leaves or in cracks. The eggs hatch in 10–30 days. The baby assassin bugs, or nymphs, shed their skin five times as they grow into adults. This takes about a year.

How they kill

Assassin bugs get their name because they pounce suddenly on their prey. They feed on the blood of mammals, such as humans and rats, as well as insects. They also carry parasites that can pass on diseases to humans. One such disease is Chagas disease.

Chagas disease is spread when a bug's poo infects a wound. Victims have a fever and swollen lymph nodes. The sickness can also damage people's heart and intestines. From Mexico to the south of Argentina, 50,000 people die each year from Chagas disease.

When assassin bugs bite

These killer bugs hide in cracks in walls and ceilings during the day. At night, they creep out from their hiding places to suck the blood of sleeping humans. They feed for between eight and 15 minutes.

Many people say that they did not feel the assassin bug's bite but the bitten area can become very itchy and swollen. Victims often feel faint or sick. They may also have diarrhoea and an allergic reaction to the bite.

High-jumping fleas

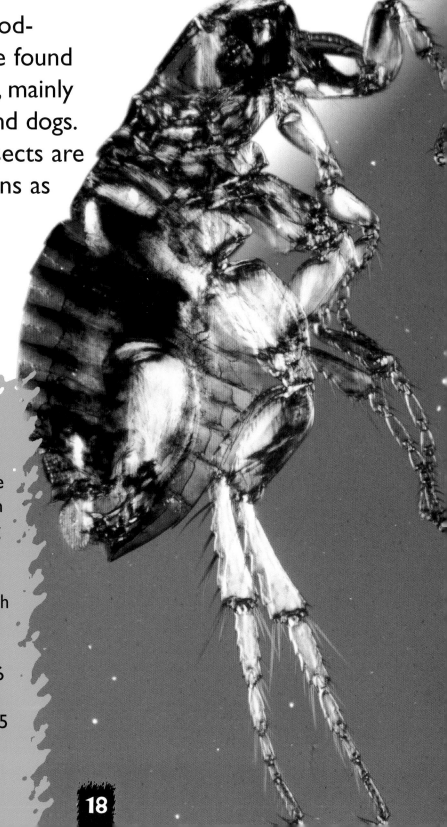

Fleas are wingless, blood-sucking pests. They are found throughout the world, mainly on pets such as cats and dogs. These vampire-like insects are as happy to bite humans as they are to bite pets.

Vital statistics

Fleas are tiny. They measure 2–8 millimetres long. They are oval-shaped and red-brown in colour. Fleas have very strong back legs which they use to jump onto victims. They can jump up to 18 centimetres high and 33 centimetres across. If a person jumped in the same way, he or she would jump 76 metres high and 137 metres across – that is as high as a 25 storey building.

Life cycle of a flea

Female fleas lay between 15 and 20 eggs each day – that is about 600 in a lifetime. The eggs take between two and 14 days to hatch. When they hatch, the larvae look like tiny worms. They spin silken cocoons that are 5 millimetres long. The larvae pupate inside the cocoons and come out as adult fleas.

How they feed

These blood-sucking bugs have small antennae that feel heat and carbon dioxide. Carbon dioxide is given off when people and animals breathe. The antennae help fleas to find a victim, such as a dog, a cat or a person. The fleas jump onto the victim and bite at its flesh. As they do this, they inject a substance to make the blood they are drinking flow more easily. The bites make small, incredibly itchy bumps. The bites can also become infected.

Encounters with people

These tiny bugs can quickly infest a house. In a month, ten female fleas can lay enough eggs to produce more than 250,000 young fleas. If you go on holiday and leave eggs to hatch, hundreds of fleas will be waiting for your warm body when you get home!

Flea bites give people diseases such as the bubonic plague. During the Middle Ages, this plague, known as the Black Death, killed more than 200 million people. Today, it can be cured by medicine.

Buzzing mosquitoes

Although they are tiny, mosquitoes are one of the most dangerous types of insect in the world. Each year, they kill between two and three million people by giving them deadly diseases such as malaria.

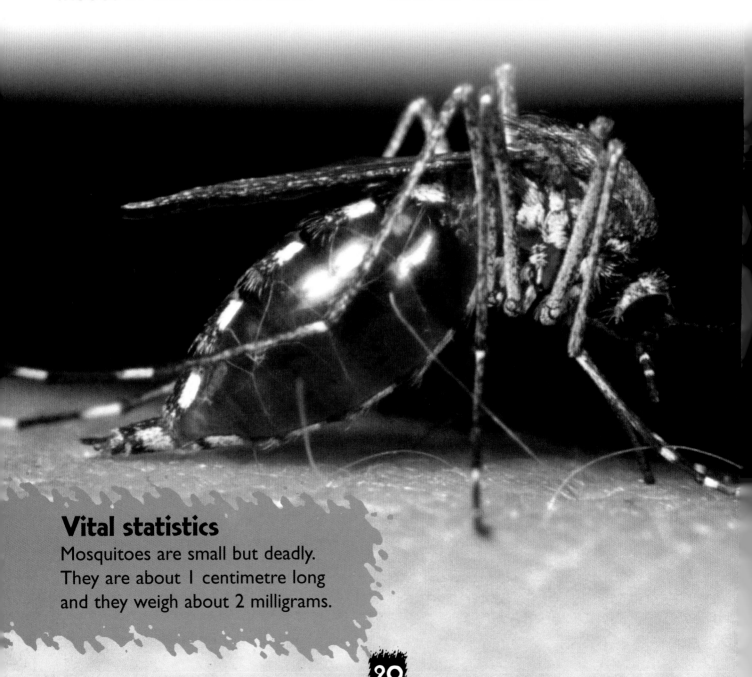

Vital statistics

Mosquitoes are small but deadly. They are about 1 centimetre long and they weigh about 2 milligrams.

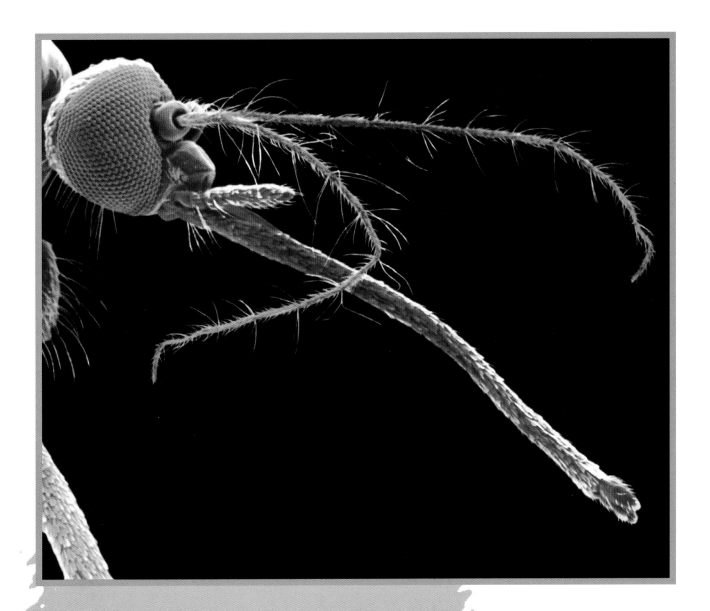

When mosquitoes bite

Male mosquitoes live on nectar from flowers and are harmless. However, the females live on blood and their bites can be deadly. Blood gives the females the protein they need to be able to lay eggs. Like fleas, these blood-thirsty beasts find their victims by feeling the carbon dioxide gas that animals – including humans – give off as they breathe. Once they find a victim, they use their strong proboscis to bite into the flesh and suck blood.

Fact!

Mosquitoes' wings beat 500 times a second. You can even hear the buzzing noise the wings make.

More about mosquitoes

Encounters with people

Mosquitoes breed in still water found in water storage tanks and drains. These are often near to where people live. In tropical regions, mosquitoes can give humans a wide range of harmful diseases, such as malaria, yellow fever, dengue fever and encephalitis. In cooler regions, mosquitoes are a nuisance but not deadly. Their bites leave itchy bumps that take time to heal.

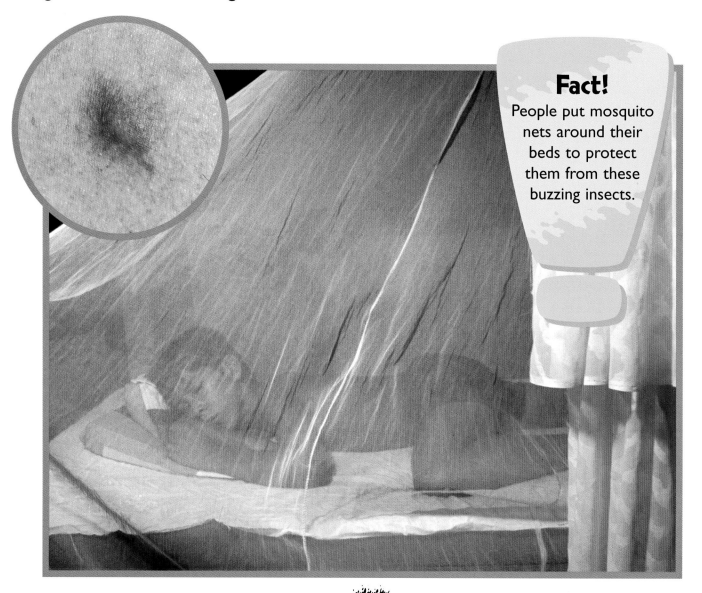

Fact!
People put mosquito nets around their beds to protect them from these buzzing insects.

Survival

People take great pains to kill these creatures because they carry such dangerous diseases. Insect repellent can help to stop mosquitoes biting. People can also take anti-malaria tablets to prevent malaria.

Some people also use harmful chemicals, called insecticides, to kill mosquitoes. The insecticides work well at first, and the mosquitoes are killed. But, after a while, the mosquitoes become used to them and they stop working.

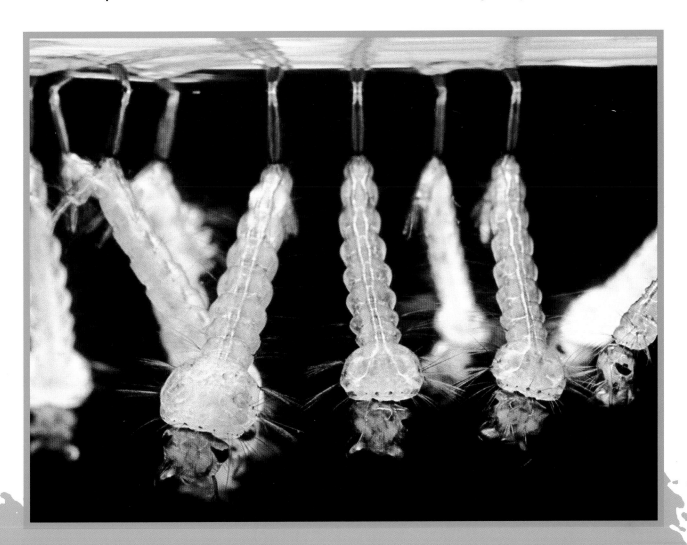

Life cycle of a mosquito

Female mosquitoes lay batches of between 100 and 300 eggs in water. They can lay from 1,000 to 3,000 eggs in a lifetime. The eggs turn into larvae, which look a bit like commas.

The larvae live under the water's surface. They breathe through an air tube like a snorkel. Once they are adults, they leave the water. In warm weather, mosquitoes can reach adulthood in just seven days.

Beastly blister beetles

Blister beetles are found all over the world. They get their name because they give off a poisonous oil that causes blisters if it comes into contact with human skin.

Fact!
Adult blister beetles are herbivores, so they do not attack other animals.

Life cycle of a blister beetle

In the summer, female blister beetles lay eggs in soil. Tiny larvae hatch out of the eggs. They wander about looking for grasshopper eggs on which to feed. As they become older, the larvae lose their legs and look more like maggots.

By the winter, the larvae develop a thick, protective skin. They bury themselves in soil and they stay there until the spring. In the spring-time, they come out from under the soil as adult blister beetles.

Vital statistics

Blister beetles are large. Adults are between 2–3 centimetres long. They have broad heads and long antennae which they use to find their way around.

Beetle juice

Blister beetles give off a very poisonous liquid, called cantharidin oil. When this oil touches the skin of animals, including humans, it causes irritating blisters. In humans, cantharidin oil can cause the kidneys to stop working and it can also cause death.

Sometimes blister beetles give off their deadly oil in hay. Animals such as cows, sheep and horses then eat the hay without realising that it has cantharidin oil in it. The cantharidin oil irritates the animals' stomach and it can even kill the animal.

Giant desert scorpions

Giant desert scorpions are the largest scorpions found in the USA. They live in the deserts of California, Arizona, southern Utah and Nevada, as well as in Mexico.

These large creatures are also known as giant hairy scorpions because of the brown hairs on their bodies.

Fact!
Scorpions may be beastly but they are not insects. They are arachnids, like spiders.

Vital statistics

Like all arachnids, giant desert scorpions have eight legs. They also have powerful, pincer-like claws and a tail that ends in a sharp, hollow stinger. Giant desert scorpions grow up to an amazing 15 centimetres long.

How they kill

Giant desert scorpions are carnivorous. They eat insects, spiders, centipedes, lizards and other smaller scorpions. During the day, the scorpions hide under rocks or in burrows. At night, they wait for prey. They use their body hairs to feel for vibrations in the air and ground. This tells them when prey and predators are nearby. They lie waiting for prey and as soon as it is spotted, they pounce on it with their pincers. Using their long stinger, they paralyse their victim. They then tear the prey apart with their pincers.

Encounters with people

Although this scorpion is often kept as a pet, it can give a painful sting. Unless you are allergic to the scorpion's venom, the sting will not kill you, but it will cause pain and swelling. During the summer, these beastly bugs may be found hiding in sleeping bags and other dark places around homes and garages.

Baby desert scorpions

Female giant desert scorpions give birth to between 25 and 35 live young. The mother makes a birth basket with her legs, catching the young as they are born. The new-born babies climb up the females' pincers onto her back. The mother then carries them for a couple of weeks until they moult for the first time. After this, they are able to look after themselves.

Ancient bark scorpions

Bark scorpions are one of the most dangerous type of scorpion in the USA. They are found in southern and western Arizona, southern Utah and southern Nevada, as well as in Mexico. Bark scorpions live in dark places. They hide during the day and become active at night.

Fact!
Fossils from millions of years ago show that scorpions have not changed much since they first appeared on Earth.

Vital statistics
Bark scorpions are small compared with giant desert scorpions. On average, the adults measure 5–7 centimetres long, including their curved tail.

How they kill

Bark scorpions are carnivorous. They eat mainly small insects which they tear apart with their pincers. Larger prey is stung first and venom is injected into the victim's body. The scorpions partly digest their prey with juices from their mouth before they suck the mushy food into their stomach.

Baby bark scorpions

Before the male and female bark scorpion mate, they perform a 'dance'. The male holds the female's pincers and twirls her around for hours before mating. After that, about 30 eggs develop inside the mother's body.

Several months later, baby bark scorpions hatch out of the eggs. The young ride on their mother's back for about a week until they moult for the first time.

Pamela the goat

Bark scorpions have a deadly sting. Each year in Mexico, a few people die from their stings. However, in Arizona, USA, there have been no bark scorpion-related deaths for more than 30 years. This is because of a goat called Pamela. Pamela is injected with tiny doses of venom, and her blood is used to produce bark scorpion antivenin.

Key words

Abdomen
The lower part of an insect's body.

Aggressive
Dangerous and likely to attack for no reason.

Antivenin
The medicine given to combat the effect of venom – it is sometimes called an antidote.

Arachnids
Animals that have eight legs, no wings or antennae and a body divided into two parts. Scorpions, spiders and mites are arachnids.

Bubonic plague
A deadly sickness carried by fleas. People with bubonic plague have a fever and diarrhoea, and vomit.

Carbon dioxide
A gas in the air given off when animals, including people, breathe.

Carnivorous
Animals that eat meat are carnivorous.

Carrion
The rotting flesh of dead animals.

Colony
A group of insects.

Endangered
When a group of animals is in danger of dying out completely, it is endangered.

Fatal
When something ends in death.

Herbivores
Animals that eat only plants.

Insect repellent
Creams, sprays and oils used to stop insects biting.

Larva
An insect in the early stage of its growth. The plural of larva is larvae.

Life cycle
An insect's change in growth from an egg, into a larva, into a pupa and into an adult. The adult lays eggs and the cycle starts again.

Lymph nodes
Parts inside our bodies that help to filter infectious substances from the blood.

Parasites
Animals, such as fleas, that live off other animals.

Pesticide
A chemical used to kill insects.

Predator
A creature that hunts and eats other animals.

Prey
The animals that are hunted by other animals for food.

Proboscis
A needle-like body part found on some insects used for sucking and feeding.

Pupa
The stage in an insect's growth after it is a larva.

Pupating
When an insect changes from a larva to an adult, it is pupating.

Species
A group of living things that can breed with one another.

Thorax
The middle part of an insect's body.

Venom
Poison or toxins.

Weblinks

http://www.giantscreenbugs.com/
Have loads of fun with these 3-D bug animations.

http://www.daniellesplace.com/html/bugs.html
Great bug things to make.

http://exoticpets.about.com/cs/insectsspiders/a/invertebratepet.htm
All the information and tips you need to keep bugs as pets.

http://www.ecokids.ca/pub/fun_n_games/games/bugHunt/index.cfm
Hunt the bugs with this fun game.

http://www.projects.ex.ac.uk/bugclub
Join a club with people who are interested in bugs.

http://www.enchantedlearning.com/themes/insects.shtml
Features loads of information and activity sheets on bugs.

Note to parents:
Every effort has been made by the publishers to ensure that the websites in this book are suitable for children, that they are of the highest educational value, and that they contain no inappropriate or offensive material. However, due to the nature of the Internet, it is impossible to guarantee that the contents of these sites will not be altered. We strongly advise that Internet access is supervised by a responsible adult.

Index